CAREERS THAT COUNT
LIFEGUARD

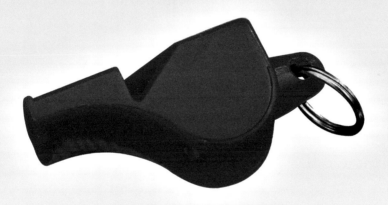

Louise Spilsbury

PowerKiDS
press.

New York

Published in 2016 by **The Rosen Publishing Group**
29 East 21st Street, New York, NY 10010

Produced for Rosen by Calcium

Editors for Calcium: Sarah Eason and Jennifer Sanderson
Designer: Emma DeBanks

Picture credits: Cover: Shutterstock: Marie Appert (top), HannaMonika (bottom);
Inside: Dreamstime: Marco Clarizia 16, Jamie Cross 12–13, Eholmes5 1, 8t, Ewamewa2 17,
G0r3cki 19, Dmitry Kalinovsky 20, 27, Roy Pedersen 21, Photoeuphoria 9, Sakkmesterke 14–
15, Lawrence Wee 23; Shutterstock: AntonSokolov 4–5, Daviles 24, EGD 15, Jorg Hackemann
26, HiperCom 25, C. Kurt Holter 11, Jodie Johnson 10, Longjourneys 28–29, 30–31, 32,
Monkey Business Images 22, OSORIOartist 2, Grzegorz Petrykowski 18, 28b, Jerry Zitterman
6–7.

Cataloging-in-Publication Data
Spilsbury, Louise.
Lifeguard / by Louise Spilsbury.
p. cm. — (Careers that count)
Includes index.
ISBN 978-1-4994-0797-6 (pbk.)
ISBN 978-1-4994-0796-9 (6 pack)
ISBN 978-1-4994-0795-2 (library binding)
1. Lifesaving — Juvenile literature. I. Spilsbury, Louise. II. Title.
GV837.6 S65 2016
614.8'1—d23

Manufactured in the United States of America
CPSIA Compliance Information: Batch WS15PK: For Further Information contact Rosen Publishing, New York, New York at 1-800-237-9932

CONTENTS

WHICH CAREERS COUNT?

There are many kinds of careers and they are all important in their own way. Some jobs make more of a difference to people's lives than others, though. Careers such as being a police officer, lifeguard, or firefighter count because they involve saving people's lives. These jobs are also special because the people who do them get so much out of their work. They help others, are creative, use their knowledge and skills, and do something different every day. Careers that count can be challenging, but they are never boring.

Careers That Count: A Career for You?

Choosing a career can be difficult. Here are some things to think about when making your choice:

- What are you best at? This can be a school subject or a hobby you do in your free time.

- What do you like doing? Can you imagine yourself in an office or do you prefer working outdoors?

- Find out as much as you can about jobs that might suit you and your skills. Reading this book is a good place to start.

Saving Lives

In this book we will look at lifeguards: the brave heroes and heroines who save people who get into difficulty in swimming pools, the ocean, water parks, lakes, and other bodies of water. Not everyone is suited to being a lifeguard. The job can be stressful and dangerous. However, it can also be exciting and thrilling, and lifeguards get a huge sense of satisfaction when they make a real difference to other people's lives. Being a lifeguard really is a career that counts.

Lifeguards save people who get into difficulties when swimming or surfing in the sea.

HEROES ON THE WATER

On television, lifeguards are often shown jogging across sandy, sun-filled beaches and easily rescuing people from warm, inviting waters. In reality, being a lifeguard is an extremely tough, dangerous, and challenging job. Lifeguards are responsible for the safety of large numbers of swimmers. They work in all sorts of situations, from busy swimming pools to cold beaches, where the ocean water can be rough and the waves high. Lifeguards are the brave people who rescue those who might otherwise drown.

WHAT MAKES A GREAT LIFEGUARD?

Lifeguards work hard to build up the skills they need to help people, but being a lifeguard is not just about training. It takes certain important **characteristics** to be a lifeguard, too. Lifeguards must be:

- Brave: lifeguards put their lives on the line to save other people.
- Patient: lifeguards may have to watch the water for hours.
- Focused: lifeguards must be ready to respond to a dangerous situation immediately.

Which of the above do you think is most important? Why?

Lifeguards train to be able to respond quickly to help people in danger.

Careers That Count: Becoming a Lifeguard

There are some basic requirements that all lifeguards must have before they can apply for the job. Lifeguards must be at least 16 years old. They must be fit and committed to staying fit. They have to be able to swim quickly and to dive deep. Every lifeguard must also have **first aid** qualifications.

A TYPICAL DAY

Every day is different for a lifeguard, but it usually follows the same basic routine. Lifeguards work a variety of hours, so let's look at a typical day for a lifeguard working a day **shift** at a swimming pool.

A LIFEGUARD'S DAY

- **5:30 a.m.** It is really important to keep fit, so many lifeguards start the day with a workout.
- **6:30 a.m.** The first job at the pool is to check the rescue and first aid equipment to make sure everything is ready to use.
- **7 a.m.** Pool lifeguards place ropes in the pool and check the **chlorine** levels of the water.
- **8 a.m. onward.** Lifeguards take turns watching and patrolling the pool from different positions. This helps them stay **alert**.
- **5 p.m.** At the end of the day, lifeguards clean changing rooms and put away pool toys and safety equipment.

Lifeguards usually work in shifts that may start early in the morning or go on until late in the evening. Working on weekends is also common. Beach lifeguards work mainly in summer and during daylight hours. How do you think being a lifeguard suits people who want to avoid a 9-to-5 routine?

Careers That Count: A Beach Lifeguard's Day

Beach lifeguards have to stay fit and check first aid and rescue equipment. They take turns watching people in the water from a tower and the beach. However, they do not have the same cleaning jobs as pool lifeguards.

Lifeguards must be fit and ready for action at all times.

SAFETY FIRST

One of the ways lifeguards keep people safe is by preventing them getting into trouble in the first place. Lifeguards spend a lot of their time making sure that everyone understands and follows the safety rules. Rules at a pool include no running, allowing just one person on the diving board at a time, and no pushing people into the pool. At the beach, lifeguards keep people safe by encouraging them to swim in safe areas of water, which the lifeguards mark using colored flags or **buoys**.

Swimmers must swim in the areas that the lifeguards have marked with flags.

WHAT MAKES A GREAT LIFEGUARD?

Lifeguards need to be friendly and welcoming, but they also have to be strict and able to **assert** their **authority** when necessary. Lifeguards may have to **scold** people who do not follow the rules. Those who misbehave may even be banned from the pool or beach for a day or more. Why do you think lifeguards have to make sure everyone behaves properly?

Careers That Count: Safety Signals

Along with calling out warnings and instructions, lifeguards use signals to **communicate** with swimmers and other lifeguards. Whistles are an important tool. Many lifeguards use a system of one short whistle blow to get people's attention and two short whistle blows to get a lifeguard's attention. Three blows mean the lifeguard is getting into the water and may need the other lifeguards' help. One long blow means everyone should get out of the water.

When lifeguards wave red flags it means it is a dangerous time to be swimming or surfing in the sea.

ON WATCH

Even when a pool is quiet or a beach is empty, a lifeguard is usually on watch and must stay alert and on guard at all times. After all, an emergency can happen at any moment and anywhere in the water.

Lifeguards may look relaxed in their watchtowers, but they are on high alert all the time.

Beach lifeguards need to understand the ocean. They know that the conditions of the **currents** and waves can change quickly as a result of wind speeds and turning **tides**. They use this knowledge to advise swimmers and surfers where possible danger spots are.

At a pool or beach, lifeguards sit up high, in a tall chair or a watchtower. Lifeguards are trained to scan an area of water repeatedly, from front to back, left to right, and in a zigzag pattern. They try to sit upright, in a position that helps them stay alert and focused. Lifeguards in a beach watchtower often use binoculars to help them watch a large area of water, so they can quickly spot swimmers in need of assistance. They also watch the changing conditions of the water, so they can move beach flags or tell people where it is safe to swim.

WHAT MAKES A GREAT LIFEGUARD?

Lifeguards may spend a lot of time in one position, but they have to be physically ready for action at all times. As well as keeping fit they must get enough rest, protect themselves from too much sun, eat well, and drink plenty of water throughout the day. Why do you think it is important for lifeguards to keep their energy levels high?

EMERGENCY!

Lifeguards may watch a peaceful pool or calm waters for hours. Then, suddenly, an emergency may happen and they have to respond immediately, and without hesitation. It could be a matter of life and death.

Lifeguards are ready to act the moment they see a swimmer in trouble.

WHAT MAKES A GREAT LIFEGUARD?

Good lifeguards must be **attentive**. They must know what signs of trouble to look for because pools can be very crowded and there may be hundreds of people on a beach. It is **vital** that a lifeguard knows how to spot **potential** drowning victims, because they do not always make a big noise or create a lot of splashing. Why is it very important that lifeguards pay attention to each person on their watch?

When lifeguards spot someone in difficulty, they must think and act quickly. They have to judge the situation, the level of danger the victim faces, and then decide what to do to help the victim as quickly as they can. To do this, they need to know all the options open to them, what equipment to use, and what they should tell other people to do. This can include calling instructions to other lifeguards and telling other swimmers to clear the area.

In an emergency, some lifeguards may stay on shore and shout instructions to swimmers and other guards.

Careers That Count: After an Emergency

After an emergency, lifeguards may interview **witnesses** before writing up a report about the event. Then they check rescue equipment and **restock** any medical supplies used, so that they are ready for another **incident**, should it occur.

WATER RESCUE

Different emergencies require different rescue techniques. In a small pool, lifeguards may throw a **flotation device** or hold a pole out to a swimmer who is tired. They may jump into the water with the flotation device in order to help a struggling swimmer out of the pool. In larger areas of water, such as the ocean, lifeguards need to use a boat to get to victims quickly. They also use the boat to transport victims safely and speedily back to the beach.

Some lifeguards use specially trained dogs to help them rescue struggling swimmers.

WHAT MAKES A GREAT LIFEGUARD?

A great lifeguard has to be able to communicate **effectively** with many different people. In a dangerous situation like a water rescue, lifeguards must be able to speak clearly to a victim, telling him or her how they are going to help, what is going to happen next, and the importance of staying calm. Why do you think it is important to stop people panicking when they are in trouble in the water?

One of a lifeguard's most important skills is the ability to swim well. He or she must be able to swim in difficult water, including cold water and water with strong currents. A lifeguard must sometimes swim among sea animals such as jellyfish or sharks. He or she also has to be fit enough to swim for a long time and over great distances.

Knowing how to use their rescue equipment helps lifeguards save lives.

RESCUE EQUIPMENT

Lifeguards who cover a wide area, such as a beach or a lake, often have land transport such as pick-up trucks, **quad bikes**, or other off-road vehicles. These help the lifeguards travel quickly across a beach with their rescue equipment. Lifeguards may use inflatable or rigid speedboats and **rescue boards** to travel across the water. Rescue boards are a little bigger than surfboards, float easily above the water, and can support a number of people at once. Lifeguards use them to paddle to distant victims. A backboard is another type of board used to support and move a victim who may have injured his or her head, neck, or spine. **Rescue tubes** and buoys are plastic and hollow, and float so well that they can keep victims afloat. They have straps that lifeguards use to tow victims back to safety.

rescue board

WHAT MAKES A GREAT LIFEGUARD?

Lifeguards need to be able to use various types of equipment. They must understand how rescue equipment works and how to use it properly. They need to decide, quickly and correctly, which piece of equipment is the right one to use. Do you think understanding how rescue equipment works is as important as being fit enough to run and swim fast?

Careers That Count: Scuba Rescue Units

Some lifeguards are trained in additional water rescue techniques. They learn rescue techniques to perform underwater **search and recovery**, using a mask, snorkel, and swim fins. They may also be trained to use **scuba diving** equipment, so they can dive from emergency rescue boats to help divers who are in trouble.

Jet Skis allow lifeguards to get to people quickly when waters are dangerous.

MEDICAL AID

Lifeguards are often called upon to give basic first aid and use life-saving techniques in emergencies. They are first on the scene of an incident, and have to deal with a range of medical problems, from broken arms and bleeding wounds to heart attacks and drowning victims.

As soon as a swimmer has been saved from a dangerous situation, lifeguards examine him or her to decide if medical attention is needed. Often the victim just needs a rest or minor treatment. Sometimes, however, lifeguards have to use techniques such as **CPR** or equipment such as **oxygen tanks** to help victims breathe again.

Sometimes lifeguards treat people for conditions like sunburn and heat exhaustion.

WHAT MAKES A GREAT LIFEGUARD?

In an emergency, lifeguards need to make quick, yet safe, decisions. They use **risk-assessment skills** that allow them to take different factors into account in a matter of moments. These include figuring out how badly someone is hurt, and whether to treat victims on-site or get them straight to the hospital. They may have to make these decisions while people all around them are panicking. What kind of personality do you think is best suited to this type of situation?

Medical training means lifeguards can treat drowning victims as soon as they are out of the water, when there is still a chance of saving their lives.

Careers That Count: Medical Training

Lifeguards must have first aid skills and may qualify as an **emergency medical technician (EMT)**. They may be trained to use advanced first aid items. These include machines such as **defibrillators**, which send electronic shocks to a victim's heart to get it beating properly again. They also use **resuscitators**, which **inflate** the lungs of an unconscious person who is not breathing.

POOLSIDE DUTIES

Some lifeguards who work at pools may also give swimming or safety lessons. These are special sessions that they offer outside their lifeguard shifts.

For swimming lessons, lifeguards need to assess swimmer **competency** and teach swimmers of different levels. They may be responsible for designing activities for particular groups, such as seniors or very young children. They must plan pool activities for particular levels of interest, fitness, and ability. Lifeguards may also give demonstrations that show the proper ways to use equipment, such as diving boards, and teach people how to swim safely. Teaching swimming and water safety helps keep people safe in the water.

These children are learning about pool safety and what it takes to be a lifeguard.

Careers That Count: Teaching Swimming

To teach swimming, water safety, or lifesaving skills, people need certain teaching qualifications. These qualifications vary from country to country and depend on the skill being taught. Lifeguards who teach swimming will not need to train in the first aid skills that most swimming teachers must learn, because they already have them.

WHAT MAKES A GREAT LIFEGUARD?

Lifeguards need to be able to speak to people who have differing skill levels and understandings of safety. One moment they may be explaining the importance of safety precautions to a group of young children and the next moment they may be teaching lifesaving skills to adults. Why is it important for lifeguards to be good at **conveying** their information or message?

Teaching people to swim is another way lifeguards can help keep them safe in the water.

BE PREPARED!

Every day, a lifeguard's job requires good judgment, skill, and fitness and even more so in an emergency situation. Lifeguards constantly update their training and skills in order to prevent accidents and to respond effectively when they happen.

Lifeguards train regularly to keep their skills, knowledge, and fitness sharp. In particular, they are required to keep important **certifications** such as CPR and first aid up-to-date. Lifeguards can work in all sorts of indoor and outdoor locations, from community pools and health clubs to summer camps, hospitals, and even on cruise ships. They may have to gain specialized knowledge depending upon the area in which they work. For example, lifeguards working with the elderly or disabled need special training.

It is vital for lifeguards to keep practicing lifesaving techniques like CPR.

WHAT MAKES A GREAT LIFEGUARD?

Lifeguards may have to tell people what to do and make quick decisions that others must follow. Being well-prepared gives lifeguards confidence and self-belief, and this makes them more assertive. This means members of the public are more likely to believe that the lifeguard can help them if they do as he or she says. Why is being assertive important and how does it allow lifeguards to carry out their job?

Lifeguards stay prepared by keeping fit and improving their swimming speed and skills.

Careers That Count: Special Training

Lifeguards have to be prepared for more than helping people who are in difficulty in the water. They must train for a variety of situations. For example, sometimes they must respond to unusual emergencies, such as a sinking yacht or even a boat that has caught fire.

RISKS AND REWARDS

Lifeguards face risks every day. When people are drowning, they often panic. This makes them behave in ways that put the person trying to rescue them in danger, too. Lifeguards at a beach face the added dangers of sea animals that can bite or sting, strong currents that can wash a person out to sea, as well as underwater **obstacles**, like rocks and sharp coral reefs, which can cause injuries.

Thankfully, few lifeguards are hurt or lose their lives. That is because they are fully trained to deal with different situations, and they have the equipment and skills they need to stay safe. The reward for being lifeguards is the fantastic feeling of satisfaction they get when rescuing or helping someone.

Jellyfish can pose a danger to people swimming in the ocean.

Careers That Count: Knowing the Law

Lifeguards must learn about and understand the **legal implications** of their job to carry out the role correctly. These include laws such as a lifeguard's duty to act: they must warn people who are behaving in a way that puts them at risk. If they learn a victim's **medical information** while treating him or her during a rescue, they must not **disclose** the information to anyone other than a doctor.

Nothing can beat the feeling of having truly helped others and maybe even having saved a life!

WHAT MAKES A GREAT LIFEGUARD?

The job of a lifeguard is one with a great deal of responsibility. A lifeguard is responsible for the safety of a large number of people. They have to make decisions that affect whether another person lives or dies. Do you have the level of responsibility and **dedication** it takes to be a lifeguard?

COULD YOU HAVE A CAREER THAT COUNTS?

Do you want to become a lifeguard?
Following these steps will help you reach your goal.

Subjects to study at school: You do not need to study particular subjects but you need to be fit and a good swimmer, so physical education is important. It is also good to play team sports or join group activities, to practice teamwork, and to show you can work with people from a wide range of backgrounds.

Work experience: You could volunteer with a local first aid organization. You will learn first aid skills and also the ability to act calmly and quickly in an emergency situation.

Qualifications: You will need to attain a qualification, like one from the USLA Lifeguard Agency Certification Program, to become a lifeguard. To get a qualification you need to be able to swim on your front and on your back for a certain distance, and to be able to dive. You will also need first aid and lifesaving skills.

Life experience: Get fit and stay fit. Lifeguards have to be fast swimmers and physically fit.

Improve your résumé: Learn about tides, currents, and other aspects of water dangers. Get to know the beaches and water conditions of the ocean or lakes in your area. If you want to be a pool lifeguard, swim regularly at your local pool and find out if there are any opportunities for you to help there.

Getting the job: When you have the basic qualifications required for the job and become a lifeguard, you will receive more training. For example, beach lifeguards might be trained to use specialist equipment like inflatable rescue boats, Jet Skis, and quad bikes.

GLOSSARY

alert Quick to notice any unusual or potentially dangerous or difficult circumstances.

assert To show a confident and forceful personality.

attentive Paying close attention to something.

authority The power or right to give others orders and to make decisions.

buoys Objects that stay afloat.

certifications Documents to show that a person is able or trained to do something.

characteristics Features or qualities belonging to a particular person or thing.

chlorine A chemical used to kill germs in pool water to make it safe for swimming.

communicate To give and receive information.

competency A full understanding of something.

conveying Explaining something.

CPR An acronym for cardiopulmonary resuscitation. CPR is a first aid technique that can be used if someone is not breathing properly or if his or her heart has stopped.

currents Bodies of water or air that move in a definite direction.

dedication Devotion and complete commitment to something or someone.

defibrillators Devices that start the heart beating properly again.

disclose To tell someone something or to give away information.

effectively Performed well.

emergency medical technician (EMT) A health care provider of emergency medical services.

first aid Help given to a sick or injured person until full medical treatment is available.

flotation device A piece of rescue equipment that keeps a person afloat.

incident An accident or dangerous event.

inflate To blow up or fill with air.

legal implications The consequences of a person's actions, according to the law.

medical information Details about a person's health.

obstacles Things that are in the way.

oxygen tanks Tanks containing oxygen, a gas found in the air that people need to breathe.

potential Something that can happen or develop into something more.

quad bikes Motorcycles with four wheels.

rescue boards Large surfboards used to rescue people and bring them back to shore.

rescue tubes Long, thin flotation devices onto which people hold in order to stay afloat.

restock To add to something so it is complete again.

resuscitators Machines that help people breathe.

risk-assessment skills Skills that enable people to decide how dangerous a situation is.

scold To tell someone what to do in an angry way.

scuba diving A type of deep diving in which a diver uses a self-contained underwater breathing apparatus (scuba) to breathe underwater.

search and recovery Searching for and retrieving equipment or people lost at sea.

shift A group of workers that replace each other at regular hours and do the same basic job.

tides The alternate rising and falling of the sea, usually twice each day at a particular place.

vital Very important.

witnesses People who see something happen.

FURTHER READING

Lunis, Natalie. *Lifeguard Dogs* (Dog Heroes). New York, NY: Bearport Publishing, 2014.

Oldfield, Dawn Bluemel. *Newfoundland: Water Rescuer* (Big Dogs Rule!). New York, NY: Bearport Publishing, 2011.

Oxlade, Chris. *Rescue at Sea* (Heroic Jobs). North Mankato, MN: Capstone Publishing, 2012.

Pettiford, Rebecca. *Lifeguards* (Community Helpers). Mineappolis, MN: Bullfrog Books, 2015.

WEBSITES

Due to the changing nature of Internet links, PowerKids Press has developed an online list of websites related to the subject of this book. This site is updated regularly. Please use this link to access the list: **www.powerkidslinks.com/ctc/lifeg**

INDEX